CH00820487

House of Commons
Transport Committee

Rural Railways

Fifth Report of Session 2004–05

Volume I

Report, together with formal minutes

*Ordered by The House of Commons
to be printed 9 March 2005*

HC 169-I
Published on 15 March 2005
by authority of the House of Commons
London: The Stationery Office Limited
£11.00

The Transport Committee

The Transport Committee is appointed by the House of Commons to examine the expenditure, administration, and policy of the Department for Transport and its associated public bodies.

Current membership

Mrs Gwyneth Dunwoody MP (*Labour, Crewe*) (Chairman)
Mr Jeffrey M Donaldson MP (*Democratic Unionist, Lagan Valley*)
Mr Brian H. Donohoe MP (*Labour, Cunninghame South*)
Clive Efford MP (*Labour, Eltham*)
Mrs Louise Ellman MP (*Labour/Co-operative, Liverpool Riverside*)
Ian Lucas MP (*Labour, Wrexham*)
Miss Anne McIntosh MP (*Conservative, Vale of York*)
Mr Paul Marsden MP (*Liberal Democrat, Shrewsbury and Atcham*)
Mr John Randall MP (*Conservative, Uxbridge*)
Mr George Stevenson MP (*Labour, Stoke-on-Trent South*)
Mr Graham Stringer MP (*Labour, Manchester Blackley*)

Powers

The Committee is one of the departmental select committees, the powers of which are set out in House of Commons Standing Orders, principally in SO No 152. These are available on the Internet via www.parliament.uk.

Publications

The Reports and evidence of the Committee are published by The Stationery Office by Order of the House. All publications of the Committee (including press notices) are on the Internet at www.parliament.uk/transcom. A list of Reports of the Committee in the present Parliament is at the back of this volume.

Committee staff

The current staff of the Committee are Eve Samson (Clerk), David Bates (Second Clerk), Clare Maltby (Committee Specialist), Philippa Carling (Inquiry Manager), Miss Frances Allingham (Committee Assistant), Miss Michelle Edney (Secretary), Henry Ayi-Hyde (Senior Office Clerk) and James O'Sullivan (Sandwich Student).

All correspondence should be addressed to the Clerk of the Transport Committee, House of Commons, 7 Millbank, London SW1P 3JA. The telephone number for general enquiries is 020 7219 6263; the Committee's email address is transcom@parliament.uk

Contents

Report

2

Summary

Despite the Beeching cuts of the 1960s, Britain's local and rural railways still make up some 12.5% of the rail network and include 17% of all stations. Communities they serve value them but most are unlikely to make a commercial return. The subsidy they receive per passenger cannot be easily quantified but is likely to be three times higher than the average for the network as a whole.

On 22 November 2004 the Strategic Rail Authority (SRA) published a Community Rail Development Strategy, setting out measures to radically reduce subsidy by cutting costs and increasing revenue. Rural railways have long been a neglected part of the network: the Committee welcomes the fact that their problems are now being addressed. The strategy should not be simply about reducing subsidy, but about ensuring that rural lines meet the needs of the communities they serve. This may involve spending money or improving services and facilities in the short term to reduce subsidy in the long term.

The SRA proposes that community rail lines should be managed and promoted locally, ideally by Community Rail Partnerships, to increase the number of passengers. The evidence we have taken has shown us the importance of railways to the communities they serve, both for business and leisure. We are convinced that they can attract many more passengers. The success of existing partnerships has shown that local management can breathe new life into local lines. However we are concerned that even though Community Rail Partnerships are an essential part of the SRA's strategy, their funding is short-term and uncertain. The Government must ensure that the partnerships have the money they need. It would be invidious to pass the responsibility for revitalising rural railways to local organisations without adequate powers and funding and then to blame them for failure.

The SRA consultation paper said that closure of rail infrastructure was not part of Government policy:[1] but the Railways Bill, presented on 25 November 2004, will simplify rail closure procedures. Worryingly the final SRA strategy document contains veiled threats of closures: "It may be the only opportunity to give many of these lines a sustainable long-term future". On the SRA's own estimates, its community rail lines receive £300 million a year – just over 1 per cent of total subsidy to the railways. They cover 10.5 per cent of the network. But it is clear that these figures are estimates, and may well be overestimates. It would be unreasonable to consider closure without much more robust financial information about the true costs of rural lines, and their true contribution to the network.

---

1   SRA, Community Rail Development: A consultation paper on a strategy for Community Railways, February 2004, para 1

1 Introduction

1. In March 2004 we decided to follow up our report on *The Future of the Railway*[2] by looking at rural railways. In our call for written evidence we asked for comments on the following issues:

- The importance of rural railways to the communities they serve;

- The prospects for innovative approaches to the funding and management of such railways;

- The prospects for traffic growth on such railways; and

- The impact of measures such as bus substitution for rail services.

2. On 26 February 2004 the SRA published its consultation document on a community rail development strategy which we took into account during our inquiry.[3] We began our work with a visit to Shrewsbury and the Marches. Journeys on a range of lines made a key part of the inquiry.[4] Officials of the Association of Community Rail Partnerships (ACoRP), train operator and members of community rail groups travelled with us. In addition we held a public meeting in Shrewsbury where individual members of the public were able to give their opinions about local services. We are indebted to Shrewsbury and Atcham Borough Council for the use of their facilities and everyone who helped arrange the visit or participated in our discussions.

3. We received 33 written memoranda. During the inquiry we took oral evidence from the Director of Jönköpings Länstrafik, a passenger transport authority in southern Sweden, Network Rail, English Welsh and Scottish Railways, ACoRP, One Railway, the operator of the Bittern Line, directors of Wensleydale Railway, the Rail Safety and Standards Board (RSSB), the Local Government Association (LGA), the Strategic Rail Authority (SRA) and the Office of Fair Trading. We were able to take evidence from Tony McNulty MP, Minister for Transport, Department for Transport, after publication of the final version of the SRA's Community Rail Development Strategy, which meant we could question him closely about the final proposals. We are grateful to all our witnesses for their help.

Community Rail Development Strategy

4. As the Community Rail Development Strategy is so central to this report, it may be helpful to summarise it here. Section 205 of the Transport Act 2000 sets out the purposes of the SRA:

(a) to promote the use of the railway network for the carriage of passengers and goods,

(b) to secure the development of the railway network, and

---

2 Transport Committee Seventh Report 2003-04, The Future of the Railway, HC 145-I

3 SRA, Community Rail Development: A consultation paper on a strategy for Community Railways, February 2004

4 A full account of the visit is given in the Annex to the report

(c) to contribute to the development of an integrated system of transport of passengers and goods.

Section 206 says that the SRA must formulate strategies relating to these purposes. On 22 November 2004 the SRA published its *Community Rail Development Strategy*, developed in the light of responses to the consultation paper published in February 2004.[5] The SRA strategy document offered a broad definition of community rail lines.

> They will be typically local or rural routes, single or double track with normally one operator, or a single passenger operator plus freight. In general, they will not include lines with significant freight flows (significant means more than 500 trains per annum) although a few such routes with strong Community Rail characteristics are listed in Appendix A. They normally serve the areas covered by just one or two local authorities with transport planning responsibilities. **They are not**:
>
> • Lines that form part of the Trans European Network (TENs routes); or (except as shown) that are designated as part of the Trans European Rail Freight Network (TERFN);
>
> • Multiple track lines (more than two tracks);
>
> • Lines with a speed limit in excess of 75 mph;
>
> • Nor intensively used lines forming part of radial commuting networks to principal cities.[6]

5. The final strategy proposes that 56 routes, 10.5% of the network, should be designated as Community Railways. The aim of the strategy is to put Community Railways on a more sustainable footing through "increasing ridership, freight use and net revenue; managing costs down; and greater involvement of the local community."[7] Some of the reduction in costs may come from new specifications for community lines. The community will be involved either through Railway Development Companies or Community Rail Partnerships, which we describe in more detail below. The effectiveness of the strategy will be tested through seven pilot projects (on six routes) which will take different approaches:

- St Ives-St Erith (Cornwall)

- Looe-Liskeard (Looe Valley) and Plymouth-Gunnislake (Tamar Valley)

- Watford Junction-St Albans Abbey (Abbey Line)

- Grantham-Skegness (Jolly Fisherman Line)

- Huddersfield-Barnsley (Penistone Line)

- Middlesbrough-Whitby (Esk Valley)

---

5   SRA, Community Rail Development: Strategy, November 2004

6   Ibid para 1.10

7   Ibid para 1.3

The pilot projects will run for between two and five years.[8]

Scope of the report

6. Dr John Disney of Nottingham Trent University provided us with a useful guiding categorisation of rural railways:[9]

> 1. Rural branch lines.
>
> These typically have one terminus at a junction with a main line and the other terminus at a small rural town. They may be
>
> (a) long (eg Esk Valley Line from Middlesbrough to Whitby) or
>
> (b) short (eg Derby to Matlock)
>
> 2. Long distance rural lines
>
> These typically serve a number of rural stations en route between two large towns or cities and may also carry some freight. Examples are the Shrewsbury to Swansea Heart of Wales line and the Settle to Carlisle line.
>
> 3. Rural stopping trains on mainline routes
>
> These share the route with express passenger trains and freight and tend to have their timetable dictated by available paths. Examples are the Hope Valley line and the North Wales line.

7. Community rail lines as defined by the SRA are likely to be rural branch lines, although community rail partnerships may operate on any of the categories identified by Dr Disney. On the rural rail visit the Committee travelled on the Cotswold line from Paddington to Hereford via Great Malvern. This is definitely rural and has a community rail partnership[10] but does not fall into the category of community rail line under the SRA definition. Shropshire County Council pointed out that some of the inter-urban routes in their area also provided important links for the rural communities.[11] Such lines may not need the same level of subsidy per passenger as the SRA's community rail lines but still offer considerable potential for passenger growth. Although the publication of the SRA strategy inevitably focussed our attention on Community Rail lines, and many of our recommendations relate specifically to them, the Committee's inquiry covered all rural lines.

---

8   Q 433

9   RR 21

10   Cotswolds and Malverns Transport Partnership

11   RR 12

2 The costs of rural lines

8. It is almost certain that all of the services we discuss are subsidised, but it is extremely hard to quantify this. In 1968 the then Transport Minister, Rt Hon Barbara Castle MP, introduced a subsidy payment for each unremunerative rail line in recognition of its social value. These payments were consolidated into the Passenger Service Obligation Grant under the Railways Act 1974, which lasted until they were replaced by franchise support payments introduced for the privatised railway in 1996-97. These are paid at an aggregated level and it is difficult to quantify the subsidy for a particular service.

9. The SRA community rail strategy sets itself two criteria for success:

- the reduction of the gap between earnings and allocated costs

- reduced government subsidy per passenger journey.[12]

The SRA estimates that the total cost of its community rail network is £300 million per annum, including overheads – by comparison, government support for the rail industry in 2002-03 was £2.6 billion.[13] But there are huge uncertainties in this estimate. As the SRA says "costing community rail operations is difficult as there are few reliable records of local expenditure as almost all routes operate as part of a larger entity."[14] The Community Rail Strategy goes on to note that "both train operations and infrastructure maintenance are generally accounted for at an aggregated level, so there is always an issue of how much of the shared costs should be allocated to any individual route."[15] Track access charges, which we discuss in more detail below, are similarly not allocated on a line by line basis. The difficulty in allocating costs will apply to all lines, not just those chosen for designation by the SRA.

10. The Community Rail Development Strategy suggests that some of the costs allocated to rural lines are inflated. It found that the avoidable costs associated with infrastructure renewal were substantially lower than initially estimated. Some overheads were inevitable whether or not lines were closed. Moreover 40% of renewal costs related to structures such as coastal defences, bridges or earthworks and similarly could not be avoided whether or not the line remained in use.[16]

11. The difficulties in allocating costs are mirrored by difficulties in allocating revenue to individual lines. There is little difficulty where a journey is limited to a single line, but when a journey begins on one line and proceeds on another, the revenue is allocated by mileage. This is logical enough, but in fact if a traveller cannot begin a rail journey on a feeder line, that journey may not be made at all, or may be made by another method. Analysis of four lines by the SRA showed that the ticket prices allocated to rural lines on a mileage basis

---

12   SRA strategy document para 1.3

13   Ibid para 1.7

14   Ibid para 1.5, p 5

15   Ibid para 1.5, p 5

16   Ibidpara 1.5, p 6

covered 11% of costs, but the associated revenue (the revenue at risk if the line was not there) was 32% of costs.[17]

Line closures

12. The ultimate way of reducing costs on rural railways is to close lines. The SRA's consultation document said that "closure of rail infrastructure is not part of Government policy nor the Secretary of State's Directions and Guidance to the SRA" and that "closures leave huge residual liabilities which have to be managed." However we detected a change in tone in the final strategy document which stated that, "It (the SRA's strategy) may be the only opportunity to give many of these lines a sustainable long-term future." Tony McNulty MP suggested, when pressed, that there might be closures:[18]

> "**Chairman**: ……….. Put simply: is your strategy going to be to get the most out of an existing asset, because you have got to keep it anyway, or are you really saying, "We are really concerned about community railways and this is their last chance to convince us that they really have a role to fulfil"?
>
> Mr McNulty: I suspect, without sounding like a Liberal Democrat, a bit of both, but probably in an 80/20, 90/10 split, given that ----
>
> **Chairman**: Which way is the 90 and which way is the 10? Forgive me.
>
> **Mr McNulty**: Ninety for the former part of your statement and 10 for the other part.

This concern has been increased by the provisions in the Railways Bill, presented to Parliament on 25 November 2004, which make the railway closure process easier.

13. Closure of rural lines would be shortsighted: they can be extremely important feeders to the main line network. The SRA strategy document pointed out the one third of Great North Eastern Railway's (GNER) passengers come from feeder services.[19] Centres of population change and lines that were once proposed for closure, such as outer suburban routes to Ilkley and Skipton in Yorkshire, are now electrified and running at near capacity. The revived Penistone and Settle to Carlisle lines also survived attempts at closure.

14. **It is only possible to take sensible decisions about the long term future of rural lines if their true cost is known. That does not mean nothing can be done now; we agree there is no need to have precise allocations of cost or revenue before taking action to reduce the subsidy per passenger on rural or community lines. It does mean that radical decisions about the closure of particular lines cannot be made without far more robust financial information. Closing local railway lines will inconvenience the travelling public, reduce patronage on mainlines, and increase pollution as passengers turn to the car. It can only be justified if it is clear that it will make significant savings.**

---

17   Ibid para 1.6, 1.8

18   Qq 424, 425

19   SRA strategy document para 2.12, page 21

3 Importance of the railway to local communities

15. The rationale for supporting local railways is complex. The SRA strategy identifies reducing congestion; supporting local economies; providing a community transport service; environmental benefits; and allowing rural populations access to the facilities in towns and cities.[20] In our call for evidence we asked about the importance of the local railway to local communities. The evidence we received demonstrated the value of the railway.

16. The Tyne Valley Users' Group summed up the range of journeys which many local railways, in this case the Tyne Valley line between Newcastle and Carlisle, can provide:

> The Tyne Valley line, which runs between Newcastle and Carlisle, is 55 miles long, and runs through urban, commuter and rural areas. It is used for commuter, leisure and shopping journeys, as well as for connections with long distance services at Newcastle and Carlisle. The line has considerable potential to serve an expanding tourist industry centred on Hadrian's Wall, a World Heritage Site. According to Arriva Trains Northern, the number of journeys made in 2003 exceeded 1.1 million.[21]

17. The view is supported by research from the Institute of Chartered Accountants, which showed that three-quarters of their members thought that their local railway was important to the business economy of their region, while two thirds said that they were reliant on their local rail service – the same weight as they put on intercity links.[22] The SRA community rail strategy also recognises the increasing importance of tourism to the rural economy.

Social exclusion

18. The railway network has been seen as providing subsidised services to the affluent social groups who are most likely to use it. In rural areas this is not so. The Local Government Association (LGA) drew our attention to the findings of the 2003 report into transport and social exclusion by the Social Exclusion Unit (SEU):

> Whilst aggregated national statistics may show that rail appears to be used predominantly by relatively well off business commuters, in rural areas this has never been the case. There, year round services are vital lifelines for local residents who do not have access to cars but who need opportunities to access employment and essential health and educational services.[23]

---

20   Ibid para 1.7

21   RR 06

22   SRA strategy document para 1.4, p 4

23   RR 15

The SEU report found that people in social classes other than A and B make 60 per cent of journeys on the regional network (that is not inter-city or commuter routes into London) and 65% of all visits to friends and relatives.[24] The Countryside Agency cited the findings of the National Travel Survey; that the use of rail by those on lower incomes is more important proportionately in rural areas than it is in urban areas: "For these people, the value of the journeys made is likely to be high and, so, it is likely that social exclusion issues will be in part lessened by the presence of rail."[25] Four per cent of rural residents use rail in any week (compared with 7% in larger urban areas). Considering the lack of stations this use is relatively high.[26]

Commuting

19. Although commuting is generally seen as an urban phenomenon, it is clear that local railways are used to travel to work in all regions of England and Wales. Several of our witnesses outlined the importance of the railway for commuting in their areas. Even the most rural lines can provide for commuter travel: Jonathan Denby, Head of Corporate Affairs, One Railway, said that the Bittern Line from Sheringham to Norwich was used for commuting and leisure and there had been a significant increase in commuting:

"The majority of the growth has been in leisure but, at the same time, we have seen a significant increase in commuting as well. Business traffic will be the smallest part of the patronage."[27]

At the public meeting in Shrewsbury there were complaints that alterations to the timetable had affected commuting possibilities for local residents, preventing easy commuting from Shrewsbury and its surroundings to Birmingham and hindering commuting into Shrewsbury itself.[28] In a debate on community railways in Westminster Hall, MPs from the north-east explained how the reopening of the Ashington, Blyth and Tyne line would enable residents of former mining villages to access new jobs in the Tyneside area.[29]

20. It is possible to support the use of the railway for commuting as a matter of policy. Mr Ingemar Lundin, Director of Jönköping Länstrafik in Sweden, told us how his county's rail policy had enabled people in the rural towns and villages to travel to work and education in the large towns by increasing services and opening stations so that 60% of the population lived within two kilometres walking distance of a station.[30]

Local transport network

21. Devon County Council told us that the permanence of the local railway could form the centre of a local transport network:

24 Social Exclusion Unit, Making the Connections: Final Report on Transport and Social Exclusion, February 2003
25 RR 17
26 ibid
27 Q 154
28 RR 10, RR 12
29 HC Deb 11 January 2005 cols1-24WH
30 Q 13

"The importance of rural railways to the communities which they serve should not be underestimated. The existence of a rail line (and a franchise to underpin services on that line) gives a certainty of continuity which cannot be matched by the bus industry. It is all too widely appreciated that bus services can be here one year and removed the next. Rural rail services provide the hubs around which other links such as connecting bus services, community transport, and taxis can be built."[31]

22. Tyne Valley Users Group took the Committee to task for not asking about the value of railways that are properly integrated with other modes of transport:

One question that the committee does not ask relates to the value of railways that are properly integrated with other modes of transport. At present, bus and train often compete.

There is enormous scope for integration between bus and train. This scope is recognised by Northumberland County Council, which has recently been awarded a large Rural Bus Challenge Grant under the heading "Bus meets Train".

The Tyne Valley railway line should be the backbone of any integrated public transport system. The route is fixed, and extra stations are unlikely, but frequency of services and stopping patterns could be enhanced.[32]

23. The Penistone Line Partnership not only runs a community bus service linking Holmfirth with the railway, it also manages a rural car club.[33] Nor should it be forgotten that station car parking plays an important part in an integrated transport network in rural areas. We heard how passenger numbers increased immediately at Gobowen station on the Chester to Shrewsbury line when the station was transformed by the building of a 100 space car park and cycle, bus and taxi interchange.[34]

Tourism and the local economy

24. Research sponsored by Somerset County Council on the West Somerset Railway which is a steam-operated heritage line, not even linked to the national network, indicated a multiplier effect that benefits the local economy. It found that for every pound taken in fare income £1.90 flowed into the local economy from associated spending by the visitor; purchase of goods and services by the railway and from local employment by the railway.[35] The operators of the Wensleydale Railway found that in their first year of operation local businesses in Leyburn, the main market town in Wensleydale, reported an increase of between 10 and 30 per cent in the number of customers.[36] **We agree with the SRA that more work should be done to identify the multiplier effect of individual Community Railways on the local economy. This would be an important lever for additional external funding.**

---

31   RR 16

32   RR 06

33   RR 13

34   Q 178

35   SRA strategy document, para 1.4, p 4

36   Qq 136,137

4 Barriers to increased use of rural railways

Lack of services

25. It was clear from our meeting in Shrewsbury that there was a great deal of dissatisfaction with the services on offer. The most cited problem was the fact that Shrewsbury was the only large county town in England without a direct service to London.[37] We were also told about poor connections to long distance destinations. Gloucester County Council has an aspiration for an hourly or two-hourly through-service to London from Hereford to London via Great Malvern.[38] Currently there is only a two-hourly service between London and Great Malvern. We heard that the availability of rail services may determine where people live, and that threats to local services may force people to move.

> "And recently we've become very disenchanted with a number of different problems affecting the railway commuting to Hereford, especially Central Trains pattern of turning round trains at Malvern or Worcester even, rather than putting them through to Hereford, and we feel that the designation of Malvern to Shelwick Junction as a potential Community Rail development may make that tendency even worse. And what it will do in effect is make people move up the line, in fact I am already looking at houses in Malvern, because I'm wondering what on earth is going to happen to Hereford."[39]

Service standards

26. A recurring theme in the comments at the public meeting in Shrewsbury was poor standards on the local railway. People complained about poor connections, dirty trains, filthy lavatories, the absence of travel information on stations and a lack of integration with other public transport.

Infrastructure constraints

27. We were given many examples of infrastructure constraints which prevented improvement in services. The most common constraints are stretches of single line track with insufficient passing loops, often a legacy of the Beeching cuts. The Shrewsbury to Aberystwyth Rail Passenger Association told us that:

> 1.4   There have been proposals to upgrade the service to Aberystwyth to an hourly one. However, these ideas have stalled because of the insufficient number of loops on the single line where trains can pass each other. Several of these were removed by British Railways during the period 1960-1990.[40]

37   RR 12

38   ibid

39   Visit Note A: Public meeting in Shrewsbury

40   RR 19

Long sections of the Cotswold Line were downgraded to single track in the 1970s to save on maintenance costs. The infrastructure can only cope, therefore, if there are no delays. If a train from Paddington is more than 15 minutes late it has to wait at Moreton-in-Marsh for the train from Great Malvern to clear the single line section.[41] Gloucestershire County Council said that the timetable could be improved by a modest investment: the installation of an automatic block signalling system to replace the token block working between Moreton and Worcester,[42] which involves the train driver physically exchanging tokens at the signal box before entering the single track section.

Competition law

28. Dr Roger Sexton of Nottingham Trent University told us that "One of the reasons why rural railways in countries such as Switzerland and Denmark are so good is that they are protected from bus competition. By contrast, one thing which makes the remaining rural railways in Britain so vulnerable is that, unlike in the rest of Europe, rural railways are not protected from bus competition."[43] A key to the success of the rural railway in Jönköping has been that the transport authority also controls the buses, which it plans and uses as feeder services to the railway:

> "**Mr Donohoe**: Do buses compete with rail?
>
> **Mr Lundin**: No. That is the reason we are responsible for the bus and rail service. We have had the bus service from 1981 and the rail service we started responsibility for from 1985. The bus service is not on long distance. In the area we are responsible for we use buses for feeder lines and city transport and rural areas without rail. We give priority to the railway."[44]

29. It appears that in the United Kingdom competition law can act as a barrier to integration in a way which frustrated many of our witnesses. For instance the LGA said:

> "We would need a change in the current regulatory regime to deliver that greater integration of timetabling and also of ticketing, and then that leads us on to our old friend the Office of Fair Trading and competition issues when it comes to delivering greater co-ordination over ticketing. The current regulatory regime is not really conducive."[45]

There are three separate issues, the deregulation of buses outside London under the Transport Act 1985, co-ordination of timetables and through-ticketing.

Bus deregulation

30. 85% of the bus network outside London is run on a commercial basis: the other 15% of the network consists of socially necessary services run through a local authority tender.

---

41   Visit note A

42   RR 05

43   RR 22

44   Q 16

45   Q 233

This of course means, as the LGA said, that unless a bus service has been tendered by the local authority, train operators are dependent on the bus operator to fit their timetables around the train timetable. A local authority can encourage bus operators to run services to stations by measures such as the building of transport interchanges at stations. But if a commercial bus operator does not want to run to a railway station there is nothing a train operator or local authority can do about it. We were told that the local bus operator in Moreton-in-Marsh cannot be persuaded to operate to the railway station, even though it is a little way from the town.[46] The Tyne Valley Users Group gave us several examples of local buses which could run to stations on the railway line but do not:

> In Prudhoe, the 604 terminates tantalisingly short of the station. A short extension would see it provide an easy connection for passengers.

> • For people at Mickley, Branch End and Birches Nook, the 602 currently passes their front door and could provide an easy connection to Stocksfield station, which the bus also passes.

> • At Corbridge, the station is south of the river, while the main settlement is to the north. Both are linked by the 602 route.

> • Greenhead and Gilsland are now left out by the 685 in a bid to save a few minutes off its end-to-end journey time. A good connection at Haltwhistle could see public transport links to these villages restored.[47]

We heard that the bus to Oswestry actually stops at Gobowen station but leaves 5 minutes before the train arrives.[48]

31. To make the problem worse buses frequently compete with trains over the same corridor. This was recognised in the SRA consultation document:

> There are many cases where bus services compete with, rather than feed local rail services, or are simply planned in isolation from them. In some cases, subsidised rail and bus services are competing for the same market.[49]

32. **All local bus services are subsidised, at a minimum, through the bus service operators grant. It is absurd for the state to subsidise bus and rail services to compete against each other. We consider that rural railways in Britain will be unable to realise their full potential unless local authorities ensure that bus services are integrated with rail. This may entail an end to deregulation in rural areas.**

Through-ticketing

33. The LGA thought that the Office of Fair Trading (OFT) would block through-ticketing schemes under the Competition Act but the OFT argued that most through-ticketing

---

46   Visit Note A, Gloucester County Council

47   RR 13

48   Visit Note A: Public meeting in Shrewsbury

49   SRA consultation paper para 4.5, p 10

schemes would be allowed because of ticketing block exemptions.[50] Mr Vincent Smith, Director of Competition Enforcement, Office of Fair Trading, explained that a genuine through-ticket is one that "enables you to add together different components of a public transport journey to get you from where you are to where you want to be. I think generally we would not see a problem with that."[51] Mr Nooman Haque, Principal Case Officer, elaborated further:

> "The other thing to add, I would say, is that one of the key considerations has to be that the two routes which are being joined by the through ticket do not significantly overlap – i.e. they are not effectively routes in competition with each other, in which case through ticketing cannot be used. So it is for routes that are, more or less, separate; for a connecting service from A to B to C, for example, a through ticket can be used."[52]

34. Mr Smith said that where there was interface between the largely unregulated bus industry and the more regulated train industry it could cause difficulties and misperception. This difficulty is more than misperception. If a bus runs from place A to place C via B from where there is also a train to C, a passenger wanting to go by bus from A to B and by train from B to C would not be able to buy a through ticket from A to C, although this might be in the passenger's interest. This is because the bus is in competition with the train on this route. Even the example cited by the Mr Haque might not qualify under certain conditions. If a passenger lives in place A and wishes to catch a bus to railhead B en route to station C then it would be most convenient to buy a through ticket from A to C. However if the same company operated the train and the bus leg this would not be permitted because it might squeeze out competition on the bus leg.[53]

Co-ordination of bus and train timetables

35. The OFT also told us that they did not see competition law as an impediment to co-ordinated timetables.[54] This runs counter to the findings of the Commission for Integrated Transport (CfIT). CfIT commissioned a consultant, TAS Partnership, to carry out a review of competition within the public transport industry, which was published in October 2004.[55] On the question of the co-ordination of timetables the research found :

> … there remains an issue concerning the co-ordination of timetables, which the Office of Fair Trading continues to regard as in breach of the Competition Act …

36. The report found that price alone was not the main determinant of demand for public transport. The key factor was the generalised cost of public transport, a combination of fares and travel time. The report concluded that it would be in the public interest if public transport operators were allowed to co-operate to produce co-ordinated services.

---

50   Q 342

51   Q 353

52   Ibid

53   Q 367

54   Q 373

55   TAS, Competition in the UK Passenger Transport Industry: A Final Report to CfIT, August 2004

37. **In rural areas, particularly, the private car is the main competitor to bus and rail services. The Office of Fair Trading should recognise this. In the short term the extent to which through-ticketing and service co-ordination are permitted should be made absolutely clear to transport providers. Once this is done we believe that the Government will need to examine the competition regime to ensure that it works in the best interests of public transport users.**

38. **There are clearly significant barriers to increasing the use of rural railways. Despite this, we were left in no doubt that rural communities value their railway and feel frustrated that in many cases its use is not maximised, either because of the poor service or lack of integration with other transport modes.**

5 Reducing costs and increasing benefits

39. Despite the significant uncertainties about the costs and revenues described above, the SRA has set itself clear targets for reducing the subsidy to its community rail lines, as set out in Table 1:[56]

Table 1

Reduction in subsidy			
		Subsidy reduction (%)	Subsidy reduction per passenger (%)
Revenue side			
Volume increase	33%	4.3	28.0
Cut in fares evasion	33%	0.3	3.0
Yield increase	10%	1.3	1.3
Combined revenue side as above		6.5	31.5
Cost side			
Infrastructure cost reduction	30%	23.3	23.3
Rolling stock reduction	10%	1.7	1.7
Operation saving	5%	0.8	0.8
Combined cost saving as above		26	26
Revenues and cost combined as above		**32**	**50**

The SRA estimates that these measures, which we examine in more detail below, could reduce the cost of Community Railways by £100 million a year. We are sceptical about the robustness of these estimates, but agree that is no reason not to try to reduce costs and increase the number of passengers carried on rural lines.

56   SRA strategy document para 1.8, p 10

Reducing costs

Infrastructure

40. The Community Rail Development Strategy suggests that it would be possible to make substantial changes in the costs of the infrastructure by changed maintenance, savings in operations and savings in rolling stock costs. Such changes would have a significant effect on the subsidy required by community rail lines.

Maintenance and renewal

41. The most significant cost on community rail lines is infrastructure (including station renewals) where annual costs are around £100,000 per track mile.[57] The SRA believes that savings "ought to be possible through a number of measures, including a changed approach to engineering possessions (when the line is taken out of use for maintenance or renewals work) and the application of changed standards." But Network Rail did not agree. Mr Paul Plummer, Director of Corporate Planning, Network Rail told us "there is very limited potential to save significant infrastructure costs as a result of the sort of things that are being contemplated."[58]

42. The SRA consultation document noted that independent and heritage railways often had lower unit costs than the main network. Mr Scott Handley, Managing Director Wensleydale Railway, explained that Wensleydale Railway managed to reduce infrastructure costs by using local contractors and suppliers:

> "I would not want to give the impression that this is the answer for the railway network or even for rural railways, but for some railways it does work. What we try to do is tailor the way we develop new stations, for example, or upgrade the track to what we can afford and what we know we can deliver going forward, but also another part of our remit is to try to reinvest locally, so where possible we plan our works and train people appropriately to the normal standards but in such a way that we can use local contractors, local suppliers, and they can work with us. That does bring costs down."[59]

43. A self-contained railway such as Wensleydale is also able to reduce the cost of engineering works by closing the railway completely and doing the work at once:

> "We are able to control all aspects of the infrastructure as well. One decision that we took last year as part of a major upgrading of capacity on the line was to close the railway for three week periods and that meant that we could provide a better service very quickly, and they understood that."[60]

This approach may be suitable for some routes on the SRA community rail list, although we recognise it may not be universally applicable.

---

57   Ibid para 1.5, p 6

58   Q 64

59   Q 142

60   ibid

44. The savings identified by the SRA will only be achieved if Network Rail is committed to them. Despite the discouraging evidence to our inquiry, there are signs that Network Rail is considering a new approach. Mr Iain Coucher, Deputy Director, Network Rail, told us that the company was "looking to find ways in which we can do smaller renewals locally with the existing workforce that we have inherited since we took that back in-house."[61] Network Rail has recently created a new post of Account Director, Community Rail. We were encouraged by his statement in ACoRP's most recent newsletter that, "Network Rail's engineers will work to develop innovative delivery solutions, which meet appropriate Railway Group Standards but which cost less. And we will build understanding of the long-term cost implications of those ideas."[62]

Standards

45. The SRA's strategy involves separate designation of community railways as a third group of lines alongside the high-speed and conventional networks, an approach adopted in many European countries for local lines. The principle is that such lines should be engineered to standards appropriate to the nature and volume of traffic being handled. The SRA envisages standards being proposed by the Department, the train operators or by a Railway Development Company or Community Rail Partnership and approved by the Rail Safety and Standards Board (RSSB). Mr Anson Jack, Director of Standards Rail Safety and Standards Board, told us he had been leading a review of Railway Group Standards which had already identified a number of standards that involved excessive cost in relation to the safety benefit and changes had been made.[63] He told us that some standards were not set by the RSSB - Network Rail had their own suite of "lower level" standards needed to fulfil their safety cases under the Health and Safety at Work Act 1974.[64] **We support the development of standards that are more appropriate for rural lines. For example it is nonsense on a lightly used line, where risk is low, for Her Majesty's Railway Inspectorate or Network Rail to insist, as has happened in the past, on the construction of a costly footbridge, when there is in existence an accessible barrow crossing.[65]**

46. **Infrastructure costs will only be reduced if Network Rail is committed to finding new ways of maintaining lightly used lines which have lower costs and are more appropriate. This may include revision of Network Rail's own standards.**

Rolling stock

47. Rolling stock leasing is the second largest element of cost on community railways. The annual costs vary according to the type of train used and the mileages run on the line but for community railways are in the order of £100,000 per vehicle.[66] In the words of the Heart of Wales line forum the cost of rolling stock is "yet another 'killer' for rural

61   Q 96

62   Train on Line, February 2005

63   Q 186

64   Q 183

65   Q 94

66   SRA strategy document, para 1.5, p6

services."[67] Lease costs do not vary much with the age of the train vehicle[68] and there was a feeling among witnesses that the taxpayer had paid twice for old trains, first when they were built by BR and now through the current leasing arrangements.[69] The expense of hiring additional rolling stock means that operators are not able to provide additional services to meet demand, although the formation of spot leasing companies for trains such as Fragonset offer new possibilities for temporary hire of extra rolling stock to meet summer tourist demand.[70]

48. The situation is in stark contrast to that described by Mr Lundin in Sweden. When the Jönköping county transport authority took on responsibility for franchising local and regional rail services, SJ, Swedish state railways, gave Jönköping the 26 old trains, which were refurbished and used for the first ten years. Since then the regional authority has invested 320 million krone (around £25 million) in a fleet of new trains with twice the number of seats, and only 8 of the old trains are still in use.[71]

49. The only hope the SRA could offer for a reduction in leasing costs of the trains used on community railways was the use of cheaper cascaded stock from 2006 onwards, as more and newer trains were introduced on other parts of the network.[72] We were disappointed that the SRA did not seem to see beyond the use of cascaded rolling stock on community railways:

> "**Chairman**: You have a constant supply of tatty old trains, is that what you are saying?
>
> **Mr Austin**: There will be the next generation of multiple units. As I mentioned, there will be the Class 158 units, by which stage they will have reached their ten or twelve year life, so there will for the foreseeable future be other sources of rolling stock that can be used quite apart from the use of locomotive-hauled stock."[73]

50. ACoRP reminded the Committee that the basic Pacer unit, the most widely used train on community railways, would not last forever: train development took many years and research should begin now. They had commissioned a report[74], in conjunction with the Countryside Agency, into a possible successor train to the Pacer on community railways:

> "....the period of time for research and development of a new train for the rural routes could be five to ten years, so we do need to start planning seriously now. We know that the SRA have already done some research on this, applying some of the principles of light rail technology to a rural type train, such as in operation in parts of

---

67   RR 18

68   SRA strategy document, para 1.5

69   RR 19

70   Q 313

71   Qq 6, 43

72   SRA strategy document para 1.5, p 6

73   Q 326

74   ACoRP, Trains, Trams, Tram/trains: Novel Solutions for Regional Railway, September 2004

Germany, for instance. But something that is acceptable in the UK environment is really urgently needed now."[75]

51. **Community railways are paying high costs to lease old trains. This alone is a serious impediment to their development. Some innovative thinking about the rolling stock market is urgently needed. In the longer term the Department for Transport must start planning for new trains for community railways, possibly building on light rail technology.**

Track access charges

52. Current track access charges paid by TOCs to Network Rail consist of variable charges and a fixed charge. The variable charge is made up of a usage charge to reflect wear and tear to assets, an electricity charge and a capacity charge to reflect the cost of congestion. The fixed charge enables Network Rail to recover its residual revenue requirement after taking into account its income from variable charges. Charges are not made at a route level; the TOC pays Network Rail for the use of its whole route network, including any branch lines. In November 2004 the Office of Rail Regulation (ORR) published an initial consultation document on a review of railway costs and charges.[76] The aim of this review is to establish a mechanism to analyse costs and consider the implementation of charges at a route level.

53. We heard from Mr Lundin that track access charges in Sweden have to be on a par with the cost of using roads. Jönköping has to pay 30% of the cost of investment and maintenance of the track in its area.[77] The rest of the cost is subsidised by the Government. We understand that this figure is based on a complex formula of social and environmental criteria.[78] Network Rail told us that ORR, in its review, is looking at the structure of costs on rural railways and apparently looking at the possibility of marginal cost pricing for rural railways:

> "**Chairman**: So could you look at a different system of track access charges on Community rail routes?
>
> **Mr Plummer**: The review of the structure of costs and charges that is just starting with ORR is looking particularly at the structure of costs and whether they are different on the rural railways in terms of the incremental effect of running a train on a rural railway compared to elsewhere, and then it will move on to whether that should be reflected in different charges for the use of that railway."[79]

54. **We support the idea of track access charges by route: for rural lines this should mean lower charges reflecting the actual use of these lines. We are attracted by the idea of charges based on social and environmental criteria and we recommend that the Office of Rail Regulation consider this.**

---

75   Q 169

76   ORR, Structure of costs and charges review: Initial consultation document, November 2004

77   Q 47

78   ACoRP, Impressions of Scandinavia: ACoRP;s Study Visit to Sweden and Denmark, August 2004

79   Q 97

Increasing revenue

55. Most rail journeys in the United Kingdom are subsidised. The problem for rural lines is that the subsidy per head is extremely high. Although increasing the number of passengers carried might not result in a significant decrease in absolute levels of subsidy it will not only decrease the subsidy per head, it will ensure that local railways serve their communities better. We strongly support such initiatives. The SRA strategy considers that achieving savings may require some initial investment; we believe this is certain to be the case.

Railway Development Companies and Community Rail Partnerships

56. The key factor in increasing passenger numbers set out in the SRA strategy is to involve the local community through Community Rail Partnerships (CRPs) or Railway Development Companies.[80] The strategy envisages that each community rail line will be supported by such a body. Railway Development Companies (RDCs) are companies that can employ staff, lease or own property and undertake trading activities in a way which is not possible for voluntary groups or for local government officers. Community Rail Partnerships (CRPs) are flexible informal partnerships which bring together railway companies, local authorities and the wider community to promote and develop the local rail service. They are funded mainly by local authorities and the local train operator which usually enables them to employ a full-time or sometimes a part-time partnership officer. They also bring in volunteers to improve local stations. Only two RDCs have been established so far; one for the Settle - Carlisle line (set up over ten years ago) and the second recently established for the Esk Valley Line. In contrast there are currently 43 Community Rail Partnerships (CRPs) which have fewer responsibilities and are easier to set up.

Community Rail Partnerships

57. CRPs have achieved some impressive results: doubling of passenger use on some rural lines; improved services and better integrated transport links. The CRP on the Cornish branch lines has secured Sunday services in winter for the first time for several decades.[81] CRPs are not restricted to the community rail routes suggested by the SRA: they can be highly effective on main lines or on TENs routes, which have rural stations on route, such as the Cotswold Line and the Crewe – Shrewsbury line, on both of which the Committee travelled.

58. Given the success of CRPs with only limited resources, it is not surprising that the Government is pinning its hopes for the community rail strategy on them. But the funding of CRPs is short-term and unstable. Dr Paul Salveson, General Manager, Association of Community Rail Partnerships (ACoRP), told us that CRPs "have had a fairly hand-to-mouth existence with a bit of money here and there, a bit coming in from local authorities, a bit from train operators, sometimes external charitable foundations."[82] The SRA

---

80   SRA strategy document, para 3.13

81   RR 13

82   Q 177

recognised that the bodies which supported CRPs tended to work on a one to three year funding scale.[83] The Minister cited the Penistone line as an example of what could be achieved on rural lines[84] yet when we took evidence in November 2004 the Penistone line CRP only had funding until February 2005.[85] We were told that two very successful CRPs had been lost due to lack of funding.[86] Dr Salveson recommended a three-way split for funding CRPs between "the train operator, local authority and other local sources, CRPs generating their own income from doing various things, delivering services as some are increasingly doing." He admitted that if the local authorities and train operators are not interested in supporting a CRP it was very difficult to keep it going.[87]

59. The SRA considered that "it would be much better if they [CRPs] were working on, say, a three to five year funding time scale which would give them a degree of security and ability to forward plan which they do not have at the moment."[88] **Community Rail Partnerships have the potential to increase the attractiveness of both the Strategic Rail Authority's community rail lines and other regional routes. They cannot be expected to save rural railways without stable financial backing. Local authorities and train operating companies both benefit from Community Rail Partnerships and should provide stable funding. Such support should be eligible for local transport plan funding for local authorities and could be a franchise condition for train operating companies.**

60. CRPs are supported by the Association of Community Rail Partnerships (ACoRP), an umbrella organisation established in 1997, before the first CRPs began in 1998. It has become a widely respected organisation and provided "extensive" input to the SRA's strategy.[89] It is funded mainly by the SRA and the Countryside Agency with supplementary funding from a number of rail industry bodies; the Association of Train Operating Companies (ATOC), rolling stock companies and individual train operators. However its main funding organisations, the SRA and the Countryside Agency, are shortly to be abolished. It was astonishing to us that Tony McNulty MP, Minister for Transport, Department for Transport, was not certain about the long-term future of this funding. He was only able to say definitely that the SRA's funding of ACoRP would last for one more year and he was unable to say whether DEFRA would take over the contribution of the Countryside Agency.[90] On 15th January 2005, the best he could offer ACoRP was a hope that the SRA could maintain funding support for the current financial year, without any commitment to funding beyond April 2005.[91]

61. **Railways are good for local communities. The government has produced a strategy which relies heavily on the involvement of Community Rail Partnerships but it cannot guarantee the continued funding of the Association of Community Rail Partnerships**

83   Q 329
84   Q 430
85   Q 177
86   ibid
87   ibid
88   Q 329
89   SRA strategy document para 1.1
90   Q 438
91   Letter to the Committee

beyond April 2005. While the rail industry should provide some funding, the Association of Community Rail Partnerships needs core funding from Government. It is absurd that the Department for Transport and the Department for Environment, Food and Rural Affairs appear unable to work together to ensure this is provided. It is astounding that the Department for Transport should subscribe to a strategy which relies heavily on community rail partnerships, and yet be unable commit itself to funding the Association of Community Rail Partnerships in the coming financial year.

Rail Passenger Partnership grants

62. The Rail Passenger Partnership Fund was announced in the Government's 1998 Transport White Paper, *A New Deal for Transport: Better for Everyone.* The fund was set up as a source of partnership funding to assist in the provision of new or enhanced local and regional rail services or facilities that could not be justified on financial grounds alone, but which contributed to the Government's wider objectives for rail. These objectives included modal shift from cars and integration with other modes. The SRA suspended the Rail Passenger Partnership (RPP) scheme to new bids in January 2003 for budgetary reasons.[92]

63. The suspension of the RPP grant was a great loss to CRPs, which had been able to use the RPP to bring in external funding. At Gobowen station on the Shrewsbury to Chester line a RPP grant of £50,000 was used to lever in £250,000 of external funding, which enabled the provision of a 100 space car park, full CCTV and a cycle, bus and taxi interchange. Ms Sheila Dee, Community Rail Officer, Chester to Shrewsbury Line, described RPP grants as a "lifeline" not only to many rail partnerships but also to local authorities who could then justify their spending on railways.[93] Ms Dee said that many schemes, had been put on hold when RPP grants were suspended: for some schemes external funding had already been allocated.[94] RPP grants also gave local authorities an opportunity to secure improvements to their local rail network through matching Local Transport Plan (LTP) funding or section 106[95] contributions from new developments.[96]

64. In 2003 the Local Government Association (LGA) surveyed local authorities to identify projects which had been suspended because of the withdrawal of RPP grants.[97] Although the response was not comprehensive, it identified some 17 projects which had been delayed, suspended or for which further development had been curtailed. ACoRP, too, said that the withdrawal of RPP grants was a major setback for its work. They proposed a local integrated challenge fund to replace RPP to support small-scale schemes which encourage transport integration.[98] **We agree that the relatively small rail passenger partnership grant was invaluable for securing external match funding: if it cannot be restored, a**

---

92   HC Deb 5 July 2004 col 484W

93   Q 178

94   Q Ibid

95   grants from developers towards new infrastructure under section 106 of the Town and Country Planning Act 1991, soon to be superseded by grants under the Planning and Compulsory Purchase Act 2004.

96   RR 16

97   Q 227

98   RR 13

similar grant should be introduced, specifically aimed at improving facilities at smaller stations or on lines with Community Rail Partnerships.

Increasing passenger numbers

65. Lines like the Bittern Line from Sheringham to Norwich show that there is considerable latent demand for rail travel in rural areas. The Bittern Line has a CRP set up at the initiative of Norfolk County Council's Planning and Transportation Department and supported by the operator, initially Anglia Railways and now One Railway. There has been an increase of 162% in passenger numbers over seven years.[99] Mr Denby told us that, in addition to the CRP's core funding from Norfolk County Council and One Railway, it had managed to secure third party funding from other bodies such as, smaller district councils, local businesses and Regional Development Agencies,[100] which had enabled the partnership to quickly promote the line and make small scale improvements at stations.

Marketing

66. People are often unaware of their local rail service and Mr Denby told us that marketing by CRPs was key to attracting more passengers on rural lines:

> "Having that pot of money allows you to more effectively and more quickly promote the line and do small scale improvements at stations, put information into places like the library and Tourist Information Centres, spread the word more effectively so that those people who do not use the railway and perhaps think that it is less frequent, less reliable and more expensive than it actually is in practice are disabused of that notion and realise that their local service is there and it works very well for them."[101]

CRPs also run special events, which are revenue earners in themselves, but also serve to publicise the line and thus generate more passengers. Such events might be station galas, live music on trains, and guided walks from stations.[102] Several CRPs have increased rail travel by introducing Local Residents' Railcards. Nottinghamshire County Council said that an increase in patronage on the Robin Hood Line had been achieved through innovative marketing, using "attractively-designed timetable leaflets delivered door-to-door to all households within the corridor."[103]

Timetables

67. The immediate aim of the SRA strategy for community railways is to maximise the value-for-money of the existing subsidy, but on some lines the potential for passenger growth is limited unless services are improved. ACoRP's comment that "Many rural lines

---

99   Q 179

100 Q 148

101 Q 148

102 RR 13

103 RR 31

have timetables which are hopelessly unattractive, with three or four-hour intervals between trains"[104] was borne out when the Heart of Wales line forum told us:

> …….. we believe that the current timetable simply does not meet the needs of passengers, and needs to be increased….

> There is little point in spending the considerable sums of money required to keep such a line open, if the train service operated on it is inadequate and does not enable people to use it![105]

We believe that the SRA's contention that "In some cases, it may be necessary to run a more restricted service until demand has grown through the work of the Community Rail Partnership"[106] is illogical and puts the CRPs in an impossible situation. Intensive marketing of a substandard product ultimately alienates potential users.

68. Mr Denby told us that the crucial factor in increasing passenger numbers on the Bittern Line was the creation of a more attractive timetable.[107] A skip-stop service was changed to an hourly service, stopping at all intermediate stations throughout the day; the gaps in services had been a disincentive to travel. In addition some funding had been obtained for evening services.

> "I would emphasise to the Committee that one of the big things in terms of making a difference is getting a service frequency and a service pattern that is attractive to the local market and there is no doubt in my mind that has been one of the critical factors in attracting more people, that it is convenient and frequent enough and they can rely on it." [108]

Passenger service requirement

69. Perversely, measures designed to protect services may now be hindering the development of timetables which meet consumer needs. When rail franchises are granted the TOC has a contract to run services set out in the passenger service requirement (PSR), for which franchise payments are made. The PSR for each route was based on the timetable in operation before privatisation. Chris Austin, Executive Director, Community Rail Development, SRA, admitted that the PSR acted as a constraint on service planning and prevented the best use of rolling stock. He set out the SRA's vision for the service pattern on community railways:

> "What we would like to do in the context of community railways is have an agreement in relation to an overall service level for which we are paying the public subsidy in support, but to allow the individual train timetables to be developed by the

---

104 RR 13

105 RR 18

106 SRA strategy para 2.6

107 Q 161

108 ibid

partnerships with the train operating company, so they would have a degree of flexibility to develop that without any nationally imposed constraints."[109]

The Tyne Value Users' Group complained that the SRA specified services on the Newcastle to Carlisle line, which did not make sense locally, and failed to meet local needs:

> Timetables are designed for the convenience of the operator, often making the service irrelevant to potential users. If the railway can't get people to work on time, get them to services when they are open, or get them back from an evening at the theatre, cinema or concert hall, then it might as well not exist. [110]

70. **Community Rail Partnerships can only market rural lines effectively if they have a reasonable product. It is common sense that an attractive and reliable timetable is critical for attracting passengers to rural lines. If the passenger service requirement is a barrier to developing such services on an individual line, it should be scrapped. Those responsible for rural railways should aspire for a reliable hourly service as a minimum.**

71. **There may be a catch 22 in the Strategic Rail Authority strategy. The franchise support payments to train operating companies will only support a certain level of service. If this service is not good enough to use passenger growth will be impossible. Passenger revenue cannot be increased without additional services; there is a danger that additional services will not be provided without increased revenue.**

Increasing carriage of freight

72. The potential for the growth of freight on rural lines may appear to be much lower than the potential for passenger growth. However Mr Graham Smith, Planning Director, English, Welsh and Scottish Railway (EWS), told us that there was potential for carrying more freight on rural lines, particularly for mining and quarrying:

> "There are opportunities for developing business served by the rural community railway. There are quarries and slate mines, for example. There is a slate mine near Blaenau Ffestiniog which is being considered for reopening and removing slate waste materials. There may be further opportunities in Cornwall with china clay and in the urban areas of north Nottinghamshire and south Yorkshire, which were previously used for coal extraction, there are opportunities where new industry arises."[111]

They also mentioned that the Bittern Line was used for freight; moving gas condensate from the North Sea.[112] The Community Rail strategy specifically allows for changes in the designation of community rail status either at a routine review, or at the request of an interested party, such as a freight operator. **We welcome the decision of the Strategic Rail Authority to exclude from designation as community rail lines some routes which English Welsh and Scottish Railway had identified as having potential for freight use or were important diversionary routes for freight. Where there is the potential for rural**

---

109 Q 319

110 RR 06

111 Q 61

112 Q 60

lines to carry freight it is important that the railway should be maintained accordingly. Community rail standards should not be a barrier to the growth of freight.

Station buildings

73. There are many redundant and even derelict station buildings on the rail network. Some have been restored and are used by businesses and community groups: such use has a double benefit for the railways; not only does it bring in some extra revenue in rent, it also enhances the station environment, encourages passengers and deters railway crime and vandalism. We saw some excellent examples on our visit: Great Malvern has both a restaurant and craft shop in attractively restored station buildings and the former station building at Gobowen is used by an independent travel agent who also sells rail tickets to anywhere in the country. We heard however that there have been unnecessary obstacles to overcome for those wishing to take over such buildings.

74. The BR property portfolio was split between a number of parties at privatisation and it is very difficult to establish who controls what. Stations were transferred to Railtrack but all but 17 of the 2,504 stations on the network are leased to TOCs.[113] Vacant station buildings are unlikely to be part of the TOC lease. Property and land, which was not being used at the time of privatisation, is owned by British Rail Properties Residual Limited, a wholly owned subsidiary of the SRA. Network Rail also has its own wholly owned property company, Spacia, which generates income for investment on the railways from the redeployment of spaces underneath railway arches.

75. The experience of the North Cheshire Rail Users' Group, whom we met at Frodsham in Cheshire, epitomises the problem. The group was trying to use a derelict station building to set up a local business. They were prepared to renovate the building and wanted the lease at a peppercorn rent. First they found it difficult to determine ownership of the building, let alone obtain permission to seek alternative uses for the building.[114] Network Rail acknowledged that in the past they had been difficult to engage with. We were told they now planned to set up a single point of contact for anybody who was interested in using surplus station property.[115] Nonetheless they considered there were three obstacles for someone taking over a station building. These were:

- Network Rail's desire for a commercial rent to maximise its income;

- The possible need for a piece of land in the future for the operational railway and therefore the length of lease available;

- A lessee's expectation that Network Rail will fund the redevelopment of the building.

76. Network Rail and ACoRP had planned to set up a Railway and Community Trust as a vehicle to attract investment funds from outside the railway to restore station buildings.[116]

113 Q 86

114 RR 07

115 Q 90

116 Q 93

But it has been decided that the new Account Director, Community Rail, at Network Rail will take on this task.

77. **The productive use of station buildings is a benefit for the railway and the community. It should be made much easier for local communities to take over and renovate vacant station buildings. Funding will be needed to assist with the regeneration of these buildings: Network Rail should treat this with some urgency.**

Infrastructure enhancement

78. We accept that the rail industry needs to control its costs, and that infrastructure enhancements are likely to be the most expensive improvements made to rural railways. Nonetheless we are concerned that, although the strategy refers to the possibility that any savings made could be used to benefit of the communities served by community lines, it lacks any clear vision for the future. We have been given numerous examples of short stretches of line, which if reinstated, would offer new travel opportunities in rural areas. The North Cheshire Rail Users' Group has been campaigning for the reinstatement of the Halton Curve, for example, which would reduce the travelling time from Ellesmere Port to Liverpool to 29 minutes. The journey currently takes 90 minutes via Chester or 75 minutes via Warrington so it is not surprising that people tend to drive to Liverpool.[117] There are also heritage lines which, with small infrastructure improvements, could be linked to the main rail network. For example the Llangollen Railway would need a short connection between the heritage railway station at Ruabon and Ruabon station on the Chester to Shrewsbury line.[118]

79. Evidence from Europe shows that investment in rural railways can result in spectacular increases in passenger numbers. The investment in the railways in the county of Jönköping in Sweden saw passenger numbers increase from 258,000 passengers per annum in 1985 to 900,000 in 2004 with a target of 1,350,000 in 2007.[119] We note that the Bittern Line, which has been much praised for achieving large passenger growth, was renewed and resignalled.[120]

80. **We recommend that the Department for Transport, Network Rail and Community Rail Partnerships should work together to identify where enhancements on rural lines would bring most benefit. They should then draw up a prioritised list of infrastructure works for rural lines which can be dealt with as funding becomes available.**

Local transport plan funding

81. The DfT provides significant funding for local transport authorities in England as part of its Local Transport Plan (LTP) settlement. The guidance for the second round of five-year local transport plans, published in December 2004,[121] states that the Department will consider supporting rail projects in the second LTP round: provisional LTPs will be

---

117 RR 07

118 RR 23

119 Q 10

120 Q 60

121 DfT, Full Guidance of Local Transport Plans: Second Edition, December 2004

received in summer 2005 and final plans in Spring 2006. The guidance states that rail projects included in the LTP should be primarily aimed at delivering local transport benefits in the context of a local transport plan (e.g. congestion, pollution, road safety and accessibility benefits). The DfT anticipates that some local authorities will wish to include proposals relating to local branch lines managed under CRPs and advises these authorities to take note of the SRA's community rail strategy. However many community rail lines cross county boundaries and the LGA saw local authority boundaries as a barrier to developing local schemes.[122] Furthermore some train operators have much less contact with local authorities than others.[123] CRPs are in a good position to liaise between local authorities and the train operator but there is no compulsion for local authorities to consult CRPs when developing their LTPs. As a result we are concerned that community rail lines might miss out on this funding opportunity.

82. **We welcome the recognition of community rail lines in local transport plan guidance but we are not sure how this will work when such lines cross local authority boundaries. We recommend that there should be a formal consultation procedure with Community Rail Partnerships when funds are being sought for community rail schemes.**

---

122 Q 232

123 Q 176

6 Conclusion

83. As the Secretary of State said, it is no good carting fresh air around the country. But that is not an argument for closing rural lines. We want high quality, well-used regional railways. It is important not to lose sight of why we need these railways. The strategy should not be simply a matter of reducing the subsidy, although that will be a welcome outcome of success. In many rural areas a rail service, properly connected with other public transport modes, will offer a quicker transport service than driving along rural roads. The Government rightly has targets for improving air quality and reducing greenhouse gas emissions: transferring traffic from road to rail will help achieve these. The Government wants to reduce congestion; while many rural railways will begin in areas where congestion is not a problem, the journeys they feed into may well end up in a congested town or city, or, if made by car, mean adding to the congestion on the strategic road network. The Government wants to promote social inclusion; a thriving regional network can assist in this. Britain currently has a net deficit of tourism; a healthy and effective rail system can attract visitors to areas they might otherwise have missed.

84. The SRA's community rail lines will have CRPs to support them; many of the lines which feed into major cities will be nurtured by the Passenger Transport Executives; franchises will always have an interest in the inter-city links. There may be a danger that the Government's community rail policy creates Cinderella services, which although important for local people, lack any of these bodies within government or the industry prepared to act as their advocate. If the Community Rail Strategy proves a success, we expect the government to look again at the way railways are categorised and supported to ensure that this does not happen.

85. Reducing costs on the rail network is important, and is as important on rural lines as elsewhere. It must be a key part of strategy. But we believe the Government should also have an aspiration for growth on the rural railway; if services and infrastructure were enhanced rural railways could play a far greater part in meeting people's need to travel in a sustainable way. We consider that any success achieved by CRPs must be rewarded with the promise of enhancements to infrastructure and services where necessary. Otherwise the Government will miss the opportunities that a successful rural network will offer.

Conclusions and recommendations

1. It is only possible to take sensible decisions about the long term future of rural lines if their true cost is known. That does not mean nothing can be done now; we agree there is no need to have precise allocations of cost or revenue before taking action to reduce the subsidy per passenger on rural or community lines. It does mean that radical decisions about the closure of particular lines cannot be made without far more robust financial information. Closing local railway lines will inconvenience the travelling public, reduce patronage on mainlines, and increase pollution as passengers turn to the car. It can only be justified if it is clear that it will make significant savings. (Paragraph 14)

2.   All local bus services are subsidised, at a minimum, through the bus service operators grant. It is absurd for the state to subsidise bus and rail services to compete against each other. We consider that rural railways in Britain will be unable to realise their full potential unless local authorities ensure that bus services are integrated with rail. This may entail an end to deregulation in rural areas. (Paragraph 32)

3.   In rural areas, particularly, the private car is the main competitor to bus and rail services. The Office of Fair Trading should recognise this. In the short term the extent to which through-ticketing and service co-ordination are permitted should be made absolutely clear to transport providers. Once this is done we believe that the Government will need to examine the competition regime to ensure that it works in the best interests of public transport users. (Paragraph 37)

4.   There are clearly significant barriers to increasing the use of rural railways. Despite this, we were left in no doubt that rural communities value their railway and feel frustrated that in many cases its use is not maximised, either because of the poor service or lack of integration with other transport modes. (Paragraph 38)

5.   We support the development of standards that are more appropriate for rural lines. For example it is nonsense on a lightly used line where risk is low for Her Majesty's Railway Inspectorate or Network Rail to insist, as has happened in the past, on the construction of a costly footbridge, when there is in existence an accessible barrow crossing. (Paragraph 45)

6.   Infrastructure costs will only be reduced if Network Rail is committed to finding new ways of maintaining lightly used lines which have lower costs and are more appropriate. This may include revision of Network Rail's own standards. (Paragraph 46)

7.   Community railways are paying high costs to lease old trains. This alone is a serious impediment to their development. Some innovative thinking about the rolling stock market is urgently needed. In the longer term the Department for Transport must start planning for new trains for community railways, possibly building on light rail technology. (Paragraph 51)

8.   We support the idea of track access charges by route: for rural lines this should mean lower charges reflecting the actual use of these lines. We are attracted by the idea of charges based on social and environmental criteria and we recommend that the Office of Rail Regulation consider this. (Paragraph 54)

9.   Community Rail Partnerships have the potential to increase the attractiveness of both the Strategic Rail Authority's community rail lines and other regional routes. They cannot be expected to save rural railways without stable financial backing. Local authorities and train operating companies both benefit from Community Rail Partnerships and should provide stable funding. Such support should be eligible for local transport plan funding for local authorities and could be a franchise condition for train operating companies. (Paragraph 59)

10.   Railways are good for local communities. The government has produced a strategy which relies heavily on the involvement of Community Rail Partnerships but it

cannot guarantee the continued funding of the Association of Community Rail Partnerships beyond April 2005. While the rail industry should provide some funding, the Association of Community Rail Partnerships needs core funding from Government. It is absurd that the Department for Transport and the Department for Environment, Food and Rural Affairs appear unable to work together to ensure this is provided. It is astounding that the Department for Transport should subscribe to a strategy which relies heavily on community rail partnerships, and yet be unable commit itself to funding the Association of Community Rail Partnerships in the coming financial year. (Paragraph 61)

11.   We agree that the relatively small rail passenger partnership grant was invaluable for securing external match funding: if it cannot be restored, a similar grant should be introduced, specifically aimed at improving facilities at smaller stations or on lines with Community Rail Partnerships. (Paragraph 64)

12.   Community Rail Partnerships can only market rural lines effectively if they have a reasonable product. It is common sense that an attractive and reliable timetable is critical for attracting passengers to rural lines. If the passenger service requirement is a barrier to developing such services on an individual line, it should be scrapped. Those responsible for rural railways should aspire for a reliable hourly service as a minimum. (Paragraph 70)

13.   There may be a catch 22 in the Strategic Rail Authority strategy. The franchise support payments to train operating companies will only support a certain level of service. If this service is not good enough to use passenger growth will be impossible. Passenger revenue cannot be increased without additional services; there is a danger that additional services will not be provided without increased revenue. (Paragraph 71)

14.   We welcome the decision of the Strategic Rail Authority to exclude from designation as community rail lines some routes which English Welsh and Scottish Railway had identified as having potential for freight use or were important diversionary routes for freight. Where there is the potential for rural lines to carry freight it is important that the railway should be maintained accordingly. Community rail standards should not be a barrier to the growth of freight (Paragraph 72)

15.   The productive use of station buildings is a benefit for the railway and the community. It should be made much easier for local communities to take over and renovate vacant station buildings. Funding will be needed to assist with the regeneration of these buildings: Network Rail should treat this with some urgency. (Paragraph 77)

16.   We recommend that the Department for Transport, Network Rail and Community Rail Partnerships should work together to identify where enhancements on rural lines would bring most benefit. They should then draw up a prioritised list of infrastructure works for rural lines which can be dealt with as funding becomes available. (Paragraph 80)

17. We welcome the recognition of community rail lines in local transport plan guidance but we are not sure how this will work when such lines cross local authority boundaries. We recommend that there should be a formal consultation procedure with Community Rail Partnerships when funds are being sought for community rail schemes. (Paragraph 82)

Annex – Visit Notes

A. Report of the Transport Committee Rural Rail Visit to Shrewsbury and the Marches 2004

Introduction

1. Those attending from the Committee were: Gwyneth Dunwoody MP (Chairman), Louise Ellman MP, Ian Lucas MP, Paul Marsden MP, Eve Samson (Clerk of the Committee), Philippa Carling (Inquiry Manager), Clare Maltby (Committee Specialist) and Frances Allingham (Committee Assistant). The Committee was accompanied by Neil Buxton, Development Manager, Association of Community Rail Partnerships (ACoRP) and Dinah Lammiman, BBC radio journalist, who was recording the visit for a Radio 4 programme, MPs Roadshow. On 21 April the Committee travelled on the Cotswold line operated by First Great Western Links to Hereford via Oxford, Worcester and Great Malvern. We are grateful to ACoRP for their help with the itinerary for the visit.

Cotswold Line

2. The Committee was joined at Oxford by Derek Potter Chairman of the Cotswold Line Promotion Group (CLPG) who pointed out the single track sections of the line. Now that traffic has increased, capacity on the line is constrained by the inflexible infrastructure. After the CLPG had taken the initiative to produce a study of the problems and opportunities on the line, a Community Rail Partnership (CRP), the Cotswold and Malverns Transport Partnership was formed to promote the upgrading of the line.

3. The CRP has commissioned consultants to identify schemes to upgrade the line. Gloucester County Council currently provides the Chair and Secretary to the Partnership and Mike Taplin from Gloucester CC joined the committee on the train. The CRP had hoped to lodge a bid for Rail Passenger Partnership funding in 2002 for a minimum upgrade which would allow an hourly service throughout the day. This upgrade would have cost £12-£15 million but the suspension of the RPP grants ended this aspiration.

4. The last section of the from Great Malvern to Shelwick junction (just outside Hereford), a single line stretch, was originally proposed for designation as a community rail line in the SRA's consultation document. Gloucester CC argued, that it should benefit from a two-hourly service to London which would put it outside the category of a community railway, we assume successfully, because it was omitted from the final list.

Public meeting in Shrewsbury

5. The Committee changed trains at Hereford for Shrewsbury onto the South Wales to Manchester line operated by Arriva. At Shrewsbury a public meeting was held in the Council Chamber of Shrewsbury and Atcham Borough Council. The meeting had been publicised by:

(a) two interviews 'planted' in the local press
(b) a poster distributed by email and forwarded to

- each Parish Council; and
- every library in the borough and beyond in a town/village with a station

This further distribution was done by the local council and library service. In addition, members of local rail groups distributed the poster in their towns.

6. 51 people attended the public meeting. The Council's own microphone system was used to produce a recording of proceedings. All those who spoke were asked to provide their name and address. Several people wrote to the Committee after the visit to say how much they had appreciated the Committee coming to see for themselves.

Shrewsbury to Chester line

7. On Thursday 22nd April the Committee travelled on the Shrewsbury to Chester line stopping at Gobowen to meet David Lloyd who runs an independent not-for-profit travel agency in a converted former station building. The agency sells trains tickets to all parts of the country by telephone and delivers them to local shops and post offices for collection. The agency derives its income from the commission from train operating companies. The companies want to reduce the commission from 8% to 7% which threatens the viability of the company. David Lloyd also briefed the Committee about the line to Oswestry (some 8 miles) which he has long promoted for reopening. Most of the track is still there and volunteers have laid new sections of track.

Wrexham

8. We continued our journey from Gobowen to Wrexham on the same line. At Wrexham we were met by Ben Davies, Area Station Manager, Arriva Trains Wales, the new franchisee for Wales and the Borders, Mike Clutton, Partnership Officer for the Wrexham to Bidston line, Alun Jenkins a local Councillor, and Dr Paul Salveson, General Manager, ACoRP. Discussion included the lack of a bus service to the station, although the station has a large forecourt and a local college very close by, and the possible uses for unused Wrexham station buildings, recently restored and available for letting. An art gallery and Thai restaurant were among businesses interested.

Wrexham to Bidston line

9. From Wrexham we caught the train at Wrexham Central station, a new station in a retail park closes to the centre of town. Ben Davies of Arriva Trains Wales accompanied the Committee. Wrexham to Bidston is one of the lines proposed for designation as a community rail route by the Strategic Rail Authority. The hourly service is operated by a single carriage train and used for shopping, leisure and some commuting to Merseyside by means of a transfer at Bidston onto Merseyrail. We saw the dedicated bus service at Buckley station which serves the town some distance from the station: the bus picks up passengers from both directions and is subsidised by Flintshire County Council. The stations on the line had been newly painted and looked welcoming.

North Cheshire line

10. From Shotton we travelled on the North Cheshire Line, which forms part of the regular hourly service from Manchester to Llandudno, and is supported by the Cheshire Rail Users' Group (NCRUG). On the train we met two of the six volunteers who maintain the award-winning station garden at Helsby, the station before Frodsham.

Frodsham

11. Frodsham also has a garden well-maintained by volunteers. The Committee was met there by Mike Collins, the Chief Executive of Frodsham Forward, the Chief Executive of Vale Royal Borough Council and the secretary of NCRUG, Cedric Green. Frodsham Forward is one of the Countryside Agency's Market Town Initiatives and also an ACoRP Gateway station. Frodsham Forward explained the difficulties in trying to rent an unused listed station building to use as a local business. NCRUG told the Committee about their campaign for the re-instatement of the Halton curve. We heard that the line is well used by 100 schoolchildren travelling from Frodsham to Runcorn.

B.Report of the briefing on rural railways in Japan given to the Transport Committee in Tokyo 2004

Introduction

12. On Friday 22 October 2004 at the British Embassy in Tokyo, the Committee met Professor Mitsuhide Imashiro, Dean of the Faculty of Business Administration at Daito Bunka University to discuss rural railways in Japan and the country's "third sector" railways.

Rural railways in Japan

13. Professor Imashiro explained that around 55% of rail in Japan can be classed as "rural". However, this accounts for only 2% of passengers, 0.9% of passenger-km, 1.6% of total revenue and 12.3% of route-km.

14. In the early 1980s, prior to the restructuring and privatisation of Japan National Railway (JNR), one third of the organisation's deficit resulted from rural lines. The JNR Rehabilitation Act 1980 allowed the closure of unprofitable lines where passenger density fell below 4,000 passenger-km per route-km per day. This density was not chosen by chance: analysis suggested it would ensure that all remaining train lines would return a profit. The government's preference was to replace unprofitable rail routes with buses, but, if rail services were maintained, JNR infrastructure and rolling stock were transferred to the new operating company free of charge. As an illustration of the contrast, densities in Tokyo can be greater than 100,000 passenger-km per route-km per day.

15. Under the 1980 Act, the Government paid local authorities the equivalent of £150,000 per km of railway closed in their area. The government also subsidised the companies which ran replacement services by meeting their operating deficits. However, the policy favoured replacement bus services by meeting 100% of their deficits; only 50% of the deficit was met if a rail service was maintained outside the national network.

16. Third sector railway companies were established to run some of the rural lines. These are joint stock companies in which public sector investment varies between 49–77%. Third sector companies sometimes used government grants to purchase new rolling stock and improve infrastructure. Third sector railways account for broadly a half of Japan's rural railways.

17. In some ways, the third sector rail companies out-performed JNR: revenue increased while expenditure decreased, and personnel costs were lower. However, in many cases passenger numbers continued to fall and local authorities often felt obliged to provide further aid to assist third sector companies. Third sector railways were more likely to be successful if they were located in cities (e.g. the Heisei Chikuho Railway, Amagi Railway and Aichi Loop-line Railways) or if they offered a short-cut (e.g. the Ise Railway, Hokuetsu Express and Chizu Express). Third sector railway companies were often unsuccessful where there was only a small market for the service.

18. JNR lines totalling 1,800km were transferred to 38 third sector railway companies. 100km of private sector lines have also become third sector railway companies. In a small number of cases, third sector operators use infrastructure owned by other companies.

19. Rural railways in Japan continue to suffer from a decrease in passenger numbers of around 3% per annum, and inadequate management. The density of traffic on many lines has fallen below 2,000 passenger-km per route-km per day. Safety standards and modernisation programmes are generally lower than on main lines, and retention of technical staff is difficult. Professor Imashiro attributed these difficulties to increased car ownership, a decline in rural population, deflation and the subsidy policy of both central and local government, which favoured buses over rail by supporting rail debts for only a limited period. Nevertheless, bus substitution usually resulted in a decrease in the number of passengers to around 50-66% of those who had previously used the rail service, and it was not viable in all areas because of snow.

20. Professor Imashiro noted that dual use vehicles had been deployed successfully in some parts of Japan. Some attempts had also been made to make stations a focus for the local community, by co-locating libraries and spas. Taxi sharing had also been encouraged in some areas. The effects of rural rail closures on rural areas of Japan had included depopulation and a reduction in the number of high school pupils remaining in rural areas.

Formal minutes

The following Declarations of Interest were made:

Mrs Gwyneth Dunwoody, Member, Associated Society of Locomotive Engineers and Firemen

Clive Efford and Mrs Louise Ellman, Members of the Transport and General Workers' Union

Miss Anne McIntosh, interests in Eurotunnel, First Group, and Industry and Parliament Trust placement with Network Rail

Mr Graham Stringer, Member of Amicus and Director of Centre for Local Economic Strategies

Wednesday 9 March 2005

Members present:
Mrs Gwyneth Dunwoody , in the Chair

Clive Efford	Miss Anne McIntosh
Mrs Louise Ellman	Mr Graham Stringer
Ian Lucas	

The Committee deliberated.

Draft Report (*Rural Railways*), proposed by the Chairman, brought up and read.

Ordered, That the draft Report be read a second time, paragraph by paragraph.

Paragraphs 1 to 85 read, amended and agreed to.

Annex agreed to.

Resolved, That the Report be the Fifth Report from the Committee to the House.

Ordered, That the provisions of Standing Order No. 134 (Select committee (reports)) be applied to the Report.

Ordered, That the Appendices to the Minutes of Evidence taken before the Committee be reported to the House.

Ordered, That the Chairman do make the Report to the House.

[Adjourned till Monday 14 March at Four o'clock.

Witnesses

3 November 2004

Mr Ingemar Lundin, Director, Jönköping Länstrafik

Mr Iain Coucher, Deputy Chief Executive, and **Mr Paul Plummer**, Director of Corporate Planning, Network Rail; **Mr Graham Smith**, Planning Director, English, Welsh and Scottish Railway

Dr Paul Salveson, General Manager, Association of Community Rail Partnerships (ACoRP), **Mrs Sheila Dee**, Community Rail Officer, Chester to Shrewsbury Line; **Mr Jonathan Denby**, Head of Corporate Affairs, One Railway, Bittern Line; **Mr Scott Handley**, Chief Executive, and **Ms Ruth Annison,** Marketing Director, Wensleydale Railway plc

10 November 2004

Mr Anson Jack, Director of Standards, Rail Safety and Standards Board (RSSB)

Councillor Tony Page, Reading Borough Council and member of LGA Environment Board (Labour transport portfolio holder), **Councillor Shona Johnstone**, Cambridgeshire County Council and member of LGA Environment Board (Conservative transport portfolio holder), and **Mr Vince Christie**, Senior Project Officer, LGA, Local Government Association

Mr Chris Austin, Executive Director Community Rail Development, and **Mr David Hibbs**, Assistant Director Community Rail Development

15 December 2004

Mr Vincent Smith, Director of Competition, Enforcement, and **Mr Nooman Haque**, Principal Case Officer, Office of Fair Trading

Mr Tony McNulty MP, Minister of State, Department for Transport

List of written evidence

RR 01   H. Trevor Jones

RR 02   Freightliner

RR 03   Bedfordshire Railway and Transport Association

RR 04   Alan D Crowhurst

RR 05   Gloucestershire County Council

RR 06   Tyne Valley Users' Group

RR 07   North Cheshire Rail Users' Group

RR 08   Ludlow Rail Users

RR 09   West Midlands Regional Assembly

RR 10   Crewe and Shrewsbury Passenger Association

RR 11   English Welsh & Scottish Railway

RR 12   Shropshire County Council

RR 13   ACoRP

RR 14   Councillor Donald G Clow

RR 15   Local Government Association

RR 16   Devon County Council

RR 17   Countryside Agency

RR 18   Heart of Wales Line forum

RR 19   Angus Eickhoff

RR 20   Midlands Branch, Rail Future

RR 21   Dr John Disney

RR 22   Dr Roger Sexton

RR 23   Llangollen Railway Trust

RR 24   David Dalton

RR 25   I D King

RR 26   Strategic Rail Authority

RR 27   Church Stretton and District Rail Users Association

RR 28   The Public Transport Consortium

RR 29   Network Rail

RR 29A   Supplementary memorandum by Network Rail

RR 30   Cambrensis Ltd

RR 31   Nottinghamshire County Council

RR 32   RMT

RR 33   Department for Transport

RR 33A   Supplementary memorandum by the Department for Transport

RR 34   Office of Fair Trading

Reports from the Transport Committee since 2002

Session 2002–03

Session 2001-02

Printed in the United Kingdom by The Stationery Office Limited
3/2005   302629   19585

ISBN 0-215-02283-1